HAL•LEONARD
BLUES PLAY-ALONG

ok & CD for B♭, E♭, Bass Clef and C instruments

VOLUME 14

PLAY 8 SONGS WITH A PROFESSIONAL BAND

Arranged by Kirk Tatnall

HOW TO USE THE CD:

Each song has <u>two</u> tracks:

1) Full Stereo Mix

All recorded instruments are present on this track.

2) Split Track

Bass and **Rhythm Guitar** parts can be removed
by turning down the volume on the LEFT channel.

Harmonica and additional **Guitar** parts can be removed
by turning down the volume on the RIGHT channel.

Cover photo © Getty

ISBN 978-1-4234-9649-6

7777 W. BLUEMOUND RD. P.O. BOX 13819 MILWAUKEE, WI 53213

In Australia Contact:
Hal Leonard Australia Pty. Ltd.
4 Lentara Court
Cheltenham, Victoria, 3192 Australia
Email: ausadmin@halleonard.com.au

Visit Hal Leonard Online at
www.halleonard.com

Good Morning Little Schoolgirl

Words and Music by
Willie Williamson

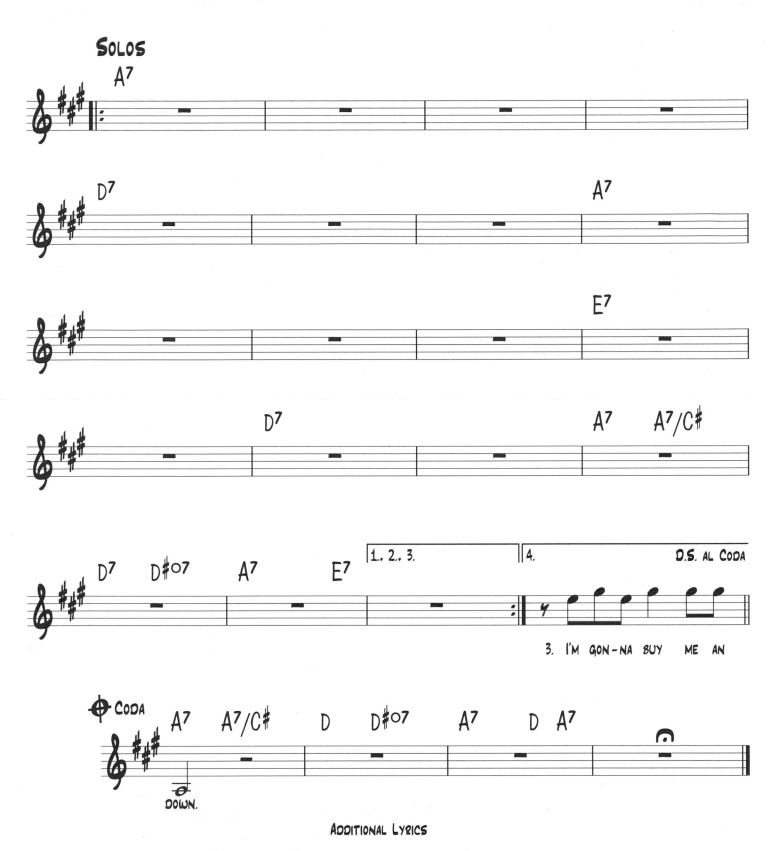

Additional Lyrics

2. Sometime I don't know what, sometime I don't know what,
Woman, what in this world to, woman, what in this world to do.
I don't want to hurt your feeling, Honey, and Muddy don't get mad at you.

3. I'm gonna buy me an airplane, I'm gonna buy me an airplane,
I'm gonna fly all over Shanty Land, I'm gonna fly all over Shanty Land Town.
If I don't find my sweet woman, I ain't gonna let my airplane down.

Optional Lyrics

Come on, be my baby. Come on, be my baby.
I'll buy you a diamond, I'll buy you a diamond ring.
If you don't be my baby, Sunshine, I ain't gonna buy you a dog-gone thing.

Honey Bee
Written by Muddy Waters

Intro
Slow Blues ♩. = 62

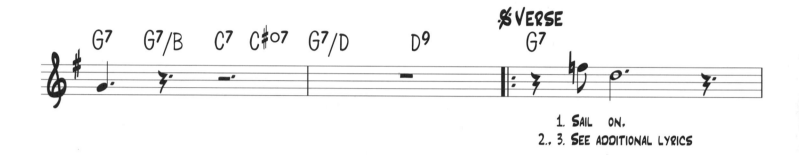

1. Sail on.
2., 3. See additional lyrics

Sail on, my lit-tle hon-ey bee, sail on.

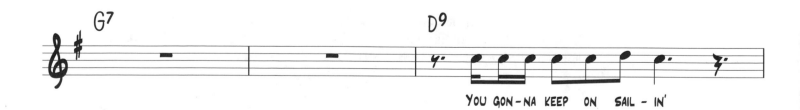

Sail on, sail __ on, my lit-tle hon-ey bee, sail on.

You gon-na keep on sail-in'

6

TILL YOU LOSE _____ YOUR HAP - PY HOME.

ADDITIONAL LYRICS

2. SAIL ON, SAIL ON, MY LITTLE HONEY BEE, SAIL ON.
   SAIL ON, SAIL ON, MY LITTLE HONEY BEE, SAIL ON.
   I DON'T MIND YOU SAILIN', BUT PLEASE DON'T SAIL SO LONG.
   ALL RIGHT, LITTLE HONEY BEE.

3. I HEAR A LOT OF BUZZING. SOUNDS LIKE MY LITTLE HONEY BEE.
   I HEAR A LOT OF BUZZING. SOUNDS LIKE MY LITTLE HONEY BEE.
   SHE BEEN ALL AROUND THE WORLD MAKIN' HONEY,
   BUT NOW SHE IS COMIN' BACK HOME TO ME.

I Can't Be Satisfied
Written by Muddy Waters

Additional Lyrics

2. Well, I feel like snappin'
   Pistol in your face.
   I'm gonna let some graveyard
   Lord, be her resting place.
   Woman, I'm troubled, I be all worried in mind.
   Well, baby, I can never be satisfied
   And I just can't keep from cryin'.

3. Well, now, all in my sleep,
   Hear my doorbell ring.
   Lookin' for my baby,
   I didn't see not a dog-gone thing.
   I was troubled, I was all worried in mind.
   Well, honey, I could never be satisfied
   And I just couldn't keep from cryin'.

Optional Lyrics

Well, I know my little old baby,
She gonna jump and shout.
That old train be late, man,
Lord, and I come walkin' out.
I mean trouble, I be all worried in mind.
Well, honey, ain't no way in the world for me to be satisfied
And I just can't keep from cryin'.

I'm Ready
Written by Willie Dixon

INTRO
Medium Shuffle ♩ = 122

Chorus

I AM READ-Y, _____ READ-Y AS AN-Y-BOD-Y CAN BE.

_____ I AM READ-Y,

READ-Y AS AN-Y-BOD-Y CAN BE. I AM

READ-Y FOR YOU. I HOPE YOU READ-Y FOR ME. _____

% Verse

1. I GOT A AXE-HAN-DLED PIS-TOL ON A GRAVE-YARD FRAME, SHOOT-IN'
2. See additional lyrics

TOMB-STONE _ BUL-LETS, WEAR-IN' BALLS AND CHAINS. I'M DRINK-IN' T. N. T. I'M SMOK-IN'

DY - NA - MITE.   I HOPE SOME _ SCREW-BALL   START A FIGHT,   BE-CAUSE I'M

READ-Y,   READ-Y AS AN-Y-BOD-Y CAN BE.   I AM

READ-Y FOR YOU.   I HOPE YOU READ-Y FOR ME.

SOLOS

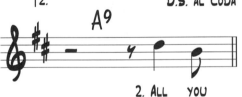

2. ALL YOU

Additional Lyrics

2. ALL YOU PRETTY LITTLE CHICKS WITH YOUR CURLY HAIR,
I KNOW YOU FEEL LIKE I AIN'T NOWHERE.
BUT STOP WHAT YOU'RE DOIN', BABY, COME OVER HERE.
I'LL PROVE TO YOU, BABY, THAT I AIN'T NO SQUARE,
BECAUSE I'M READY, AS READY'S ANYBODY CAN BE.
I AM READY FOR YOU, I HOPE YOU READY FOR ME.

Optional Lyrics

I BEEN DRINKIN' GIN LIKE NEVER BEFORE.
I FEEL SO GOOD THAT I WANT YOU TO KNOW.
ONE MORE DRINK, I WISH YOU WOULD.
IT TAKE A WHOLE LOT OF LOVIN' TO MAKE ME FEEL GOOD.
WELL, I'M READY, AS READY'S ANYBODY CAN BE.
I AM READY FOR YOU, I HOPE YOU READY FOR ME.

C Version

Mannish Boy
Written by Muddy Waters, Melvin London and Ellas McDaniel

"N." ___   THAT REP-RE-SENT MAN.   NO "B." ___

"O," ___ CHILD. ___   "Y," ___   THAT SPELL MAN-NISH BOY.

I'M A MAN. ___   I'M A FULL-GROWN MAN.

I'M A MAN. ___   I'M A ROLL - IN' STONE.

I'M A MAN. ___   I'M A HOOCH-IE COOCH-IE MAN.

VERSE
A7

2. SIT-TIN' ON THE OUT - SIDE,   JUST ME AND MY MATE.

I MADE THE MOON   COME UP TWO HOURS ___ LATE.

Trouble No More
(Someday Baby)
Written by Muddy Waters

INTRO
MODERATE SHUFFLE ♩ = 153

VERSE

1. Don't care how long you go.
2., 3. See additional lyrics

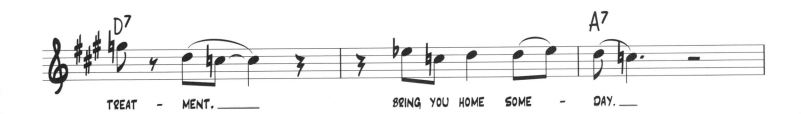

I don't care how long you stay. ___ But good. kind

TREAT - MENT, ___ Bring you home some - day. ___

But some - day ba - by, you ain't gon-na trou - ble ___ poor ___

ME AN - Y - MORE.

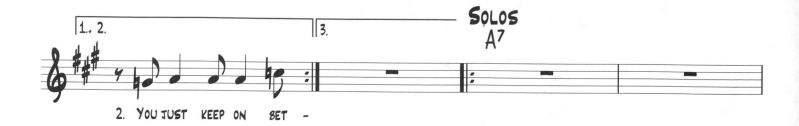

SOLOS

A7

2. YOU JUST KEEP ON BET -

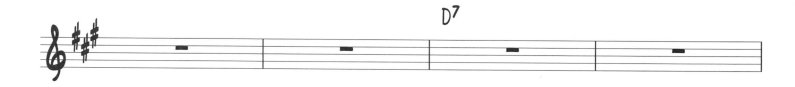

D7

A7

1., 2., 3.

VERSE

A7

4. I'M GON - NA TELL EV - 'RY - BOD - Y   IN YOUR NEIGH - BOR - HOOD

5., 6. SEE ADDITIONAL LYRICS

D7

THAT YOU'RE A SWEET LIT - TLE GIRL

BUT YOU DON'T ___ MEAN ME NO GOOD.

BUT SOME - DAY, BA - BY, YOU AIN'T GON - NA

TROU - BLE ___ POOR ___ ME ___ AN - Y - MORE.

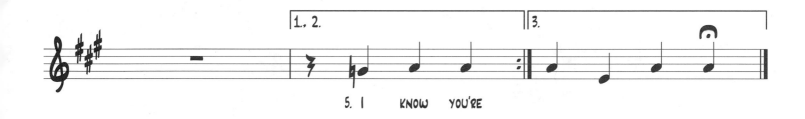

1, 2.   3.

5. I KNOW YOU'RE

Additional Lyrics

2. You just keep on bettin'
That the dice won't pass.
Well you know, darlin'
You are livin' too fast.
But someday, baby,
you ain't gonna trouble
Poor me anymore.

3. I'm gonna tell ev'rybody
In your neighborhood
That you're a sweet little girl
But you don't mean me no good.
But someday, baby,
you ain't gonna trouble
Poor me anymore.

5. I know you're leaving.
You call that gone.
Oh, without my love
You can't stay long.
But someday, baby,
You ain't gonna trouble
Poor me anymore.

6. Well, goodbye, baby.
Come on, shake my hand.
I don't want no woman
You can have a man.
But someday, baby,
You ain't gonna trouble
Poor me anymore.

Rollin' Stone
(Catfish Blues)
Written by Muddy Waters

Slow Blues ♩. = 67

1. Well I wish ___ I was a cat - fish swim-min' in
2., 3. See additional lyrics

a whole ___ deep blue sea. ___ I will have all

you good look - in' wom-en ___ fish - in', fish - in' af - ter me.

Sure 'nough ___ af - ter me. Sure 'nough ___ af - ter me. ___

Oh, Lord. ___ Oh, Lord. ___

Sure 'nough. ___

To Coda ⊕

2. I went to ___

Additional Lyrics

2. I went to my baby's house
   And I sit down, ho, on her step.
   She said, "Come on in, now, Muddy.
   You know my husband just now left.
   Sure enough, he just now left.
   Sure enough, he just now left."
   Oh, Lord. Oh well, oh well.

3. Well, I feel, yes, I feel,
   Baby, like the low down, ho, time ain't long.
   I'm gonna catch the first thing smokin',
   Back, back down the road I'm going.
   Back down the road I'm going.
   Back down the road I'm going.
   Sure enough, eh. Sure enough, eh.

Optional Lyrics

Well, my mother told my father
Just before, hmm, I was born,
"I got a boy child's comin'
He's gonna be a rollin' stone.
Sure enough, he's a rollin' stone.
Sure enough, he's a rollin' stone.
Oh well he's a, oh well he's a, oh well he's a."

You Shook Me

Words and Music by Willie Dixon and J.B. Lenoir

Intro
Slow Blues ♩. = 68

1. You know you shook me, ba - by.
2., 3. See additional lyrics

You shook me all ____ night long. ____

You know you shook me, ba - by.

You shook me all ____ night long. ____

ADDITIONAL LYRICS

2. YOU KNOW YOU MOVE ME, BABY,
   JUST LIKE A HURRICANE.
   YOU KNOW YOU MOVED ME, BABY,
   JUST LIKE A HURRICANE.
   OH, YOU KNOW YOU MOVE ME, DARLING,
   JUST LIKE AN EARTHQUAKE MOVES THE LAND.

3. OH, SOMETIME I WONDER
   WHAT MY POOR WIFE AND CHILD'S GONNA DO.
   OH, SOMETIME I WONDER
   WHAT MY POOR WIFE AND CHILD'S GONNA DO.
   OH, YOU KNOW YOU MADE ME MISTREAT THEM, DARLING.
   OH, I'M MADLY IN LOVE WITH YOU.

SOLOS

3. I'M GON-NA BUY ME AN

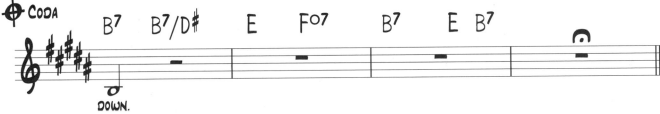

DOWN.

ADDITIONAL LYRICS

2. Sometime I don't know what, sometime I don't know what,
   Woman, what in this world to, woman, what in this world to do.
   I don't want to hurt your feeling, Honey, and Muddy don't get mad at you.

3. I'm gonna buy me an airplane, I'm gonna buy me an airplane,
   I'm gonna fly all over Shanty Land, I'm gonna fly all over Shanty Land Town.
   If I don't find my sweet woman, I ain't gonna let my airplane down.

OPTIONAL LYRICS

Come on, be my baby. Come on, be my baby.
I'll buy you a diamond, I'll buy you a diamond ring.
If you don't be my baby, Sunshine, I ain't gonna buy you a dog-gone thing.

Honey Bee
Written by Muddy Waters

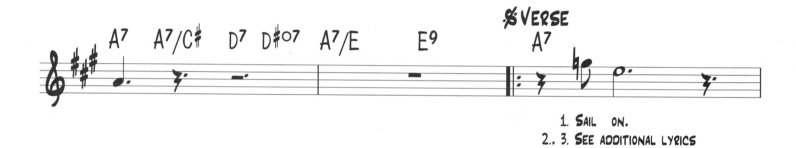

1. Sail on.
2., 3. See additional lyrics

Sail on, my lit-tle hon-ey bee, sail on.

Sail on, Sail ___ on, my lit-tle hon-ey bee, sail on.

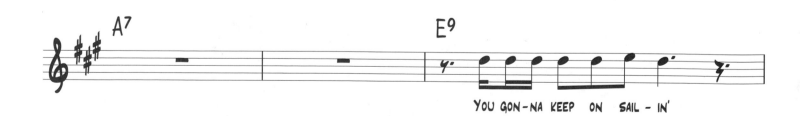

You gon-na keep on sail-in'

TILLYOU LOSE _____ YOUR HAP - PY HOME.

SOLOS

2ND TIME, D.S. AL CODA

ADDITIONAL LYRICS

2. SAIL ON, SAIL ON, MY LITTLE HONEY BEE, SAIL ON.
   SAIL ON, SAIL ON, MY LITTLE HONEY BEE, SAIL ON.
   I DON'T MIND YOU SAILIN', BUT PLEASE DON'T SAIL SO LONG.
   ALL RIGHT, LITTLE HONEY BEE.

3. I HEAR A LOT OF BUZZING. SOUNDS LIKE MY LITTLE HONEY BEE.
   I HEAR A LOT OF BUZZING. SOUNDS LIKE MY LITTLE HONEY BEE.
   SHE BEEN ALL AROUND THE WORLD MAKIN' HONEY,
   BUT NOW SHE IS COMIN' BACK HOME TO ME.

I Can't Be Satisfied

Written by Muddy Waters

Additional Lyrics

2. Well, I feel like snappin'
   Pistol in your face.
   I'm gonna let some graveyard
   Lord, be her resting place.
   Woman, I'm troubled, I be all worried in mind.
   Well, baby, I can never be satisfied
   And I just can't keep from cryin'.

3. Well, now, all in my sleep,
   Hear my doorbell ring.
   Lookin' for my baby,
   I didn't see not a dog-gone thing.
   I was troubled, I was all worried in mind.
   Well, honey, I could never be satisfied
   And I just couldn't keep from cryin'.

Optional Lyrics

Well, I know my little old baby,
She gonna jump and shout.
That old train be late, man,
Lord, and I come walkin' out.
I mean trouble, I be all worried in mind.
Well, honey, ain't no way in the world for me to be satisfied
And I just can't keep from cryin'.

I'm Ready
Written by Willie Dixon

Lyrics under the staff:

DY - NA - MITE. I HOPE SOME __ SCREW-BALL START A FIGHT, BE-CAUSE I'M

READ-Y, READ-Y AS AN - Y - BOD - Y CAN BE. I AM

READ-Y FOR YOU. I HOPE YOU READ-Y FOR ME.

Solos

2. ALL YOU

Additional Lyrics

2. All you pretty little chicks with your curly hair,
I know you feel like I ain't nowhere.
But stop what you're doin', baby, come over here.
I'll prove to you, baby, that I ain't no square.
Because I'm ready, as ready's anybody can be.
I am ready for you, I hope you ready for me.

Optional Lyrics

I been drinkin' gin like never before.
I feel so good that I want you to know.
One more drink, I wish you would.
It take a whole lot of lovin' to make me feel good.
Well, I'm ready, as ready's anybody can be.
I am ready for you, I hope you ready for me.

B♭ Version

Mannish Boy
Written by Muddy Waters, Melvin London and Ellas McDaniel

INTRO
Shuffle ♩. = 70

VERSE

1. Now when I was young boy, at the age of five,

My moth-er said I'm gon-na be ___ the great-est man a-live.

But now I'm a man. ___ I made twen-ty-one. ___

I want you be-lieve me, hon-ey, we have lots of fun.

I'm a man. I spell "M." ___ "A." ___ child, ___

TROUBLE NO MORE
(SOMEDAY BABY)
WRITTEN BY MUDDY WATERS

INTRO
MODERATE SHUFFLE ♩ = 153

1. DON'T CARE HOW LONG YOU GO.

2. 3. SEE ADDITIONAL LYRICS

I DON'T CARE HOW LONG YOU STAY. ___ BUT GOOD, KIND

TREAT - MENT. ___ BRING YOU HOME SOME - DAY. ___

BUT SOME - DAY BA - BY, YOU AIN'T GON-NA TROU - BLE ___ POOR ___

ME AN - Y - MORE.

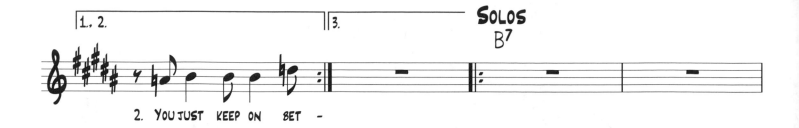

1., 2.   3.   **SOLOS**
B7

2. YOU JUST KEEP ON BET -

E7

B7

1., 2., 3.

4.   **VERSE**
B7

4. I'M GON - NA TELL EV - 'RY - BOD - Y   IN YOUR NEIGH - BOR - HOOD
5., 6. SEE ADDITIONAL LYRICS

E7

THAT YOU'RE A SWEET LIT - TLE GIRL

BUT YOU DON'T ____ MEAN ME NO GOOD.

BUT SOME - DAY, BA - BY, YOU AIN'T GON - NA

TROU - BLE ____ POOR ____ ME ____ AN - Y - MORE.

5. I KNOW YOU'RE

Additional Lyrics

2. You just keep on bettin'
   That the dice won't pass.
   Well you know, darlin'
   You are livin' too fast.
   But someday, baby,
   You ain't gonna trouble
   Poor me anymore.

3. I'm gonna tell ev'rybody
   In your neighborhood
   That you're a sweet little girl
   But you don't mean me no good.
   But someday, baby,
   You ain't gonna trouble
   Poor me anymore.

5. I know you're leaving.
   You call that gone.
   Oh, without my love
   You can't stay long.
   But someday, baby,
   You ain't gonna trouble
   Poor me anymore.

6. Well, goodbye, baby.
   Come on, shake my hand.
   I don't want no woman
   You can have a man.
   But someday, baby,
   You ain't gonna trouble
   Poor me anymore.

Rollin' Stone
(Catfish Blues)
Written by Muddy Waters

Additional Lyrics

2. I WENT TO MY BABY'S HOUSE
   AND I SIT DOWN, HO, ON HER STEP.
   SHE SAID, "COME ON IN, NOW, MUDDY.
   YOU KNOW MY HUSBAND JUST NOW LEFT.
   SURE ENOUGH, HE JUST NOW LEFT.
   SURE ENOUGH, HE JUST NOW LEFT."
   OH, LORD. OH WELL, OH WELL.

3. WELL, I FEEL, YES, I FEEL,
   BABY, LIKE THE LOW DOWN, HO, TIME AIN'T LONG.
   I'M GONNA CATCH THE FIRST THING SMOKIN'.
   BACK, BACK DOWN THE ROAD I'M GOING.
   BACK DOWN THE ROAD I'M GOING.
   BACK DOWN THE ROAD I'M GOING.
   SURE ENOUGH, EH. SURE ENOUGH, EH.

Optional Lyrics

WELL, MY MOTHER TOLD MY FATHER
JUST BEFORE, HMM, I WAS BORN,
"I GOT A BOY CHILD'S COMIN'
HE'S GONNA BE A ROLLIN' STONE.
SURE ENOUGH, HE'S A ROLLIN' STONE.
SURE ENOUGH, HE'S A ROLLIN' STONE.
OH WELL HE'S A, OH WELL HE'S A, OH WELL HE'S A."

You Shook Me

Words and Music by Willie Dixon and J.B. Lenoir

1. You know you shook me, ba - by.

2., 3. See additional lyrics

You shook me all ___ night long. ___

You know you shook me, ba - by.

You shook me all ___ night long. ___

Additional Lyrics

2. You know you move me, baby,
   Just like a hurricane.
   You know you moved me, baby,
   Just like a hurricane.
   Oh, you know you move me, darling,
   Just like an earthquake moves the land.

3. Oh, sometime I wonder
   What my poor wife and child's gonna do.
   Oh, sometime I wonder
   What my poor wife and child's gonna do.
   Oh, you know you made me mistreat them, darling.
   Oh, I'm madly in love with you.

Good Morning Little Schoolgirl

Words and Music by
Willie Williamson

Solos

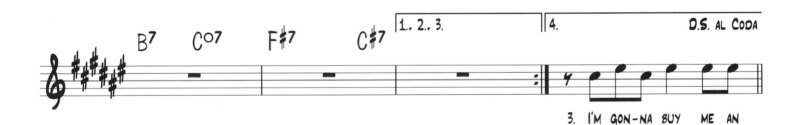

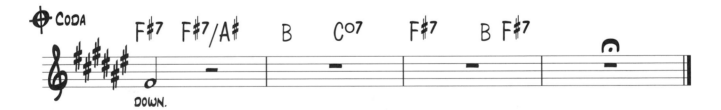

Additional Lyrics

2. Sometime I don't know what, sometime I don't know what,
Woman, what in this world to, woman, what in this world to do.
I don't want to hurt your feeling, Honey, and Muddy don't get mad at you.

3. I'm gonna buy me an airplane, I'm gonna buy me an airplane.
I'm gonna fly all over Shanty Land, I'm gonna fly all over Shanty Land Town.
If I don't find my sweet woman, I ain't gonna let my airplane down.

Optional Lyrics

Come on, be my baby. Come on, be my baby.
I'll buy you a diamond, I'll buy you a diamond ring.
If you don't be my baby, Sunshine, I ain't gonna buy you a dog-gone thing.

CD TRACK

② Full Stereo Mix

⑩ Split Mix

E♭ Version

Honey Bee

Written by Muddy Waters

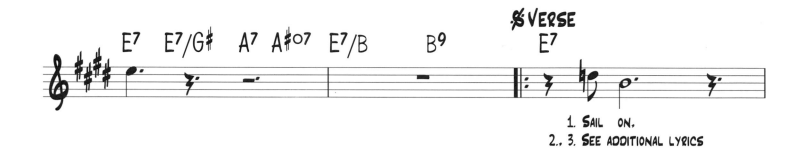

SAIL ON, MY LIT-TLE HON-EY BEE, SAIL ON.

SAIL ON,   SAIL ___ ON, MY LIT-TLE HON-EY BEE, SAIL ON.

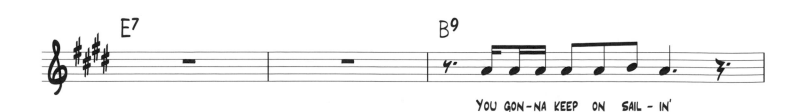

YOU GON-NA KEEP ON SAIL-IN'

TILL YOU LOSE _____ YOUR HAP-PY HOME.

SOLOS

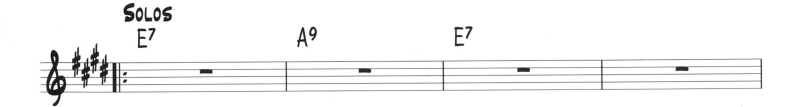

ADDITIONAL LYRICS

2. SAIL ON, SAIL ON, MY LITTLE HONEY BEE, SAIL ON.
   SAIL ON, SAIL ON, MY LITTLE HONEY BEE, SAIL ON.
   I DON'T MIND YOU SAILIN', BUT PLEASE DON'T SAIL SO LONG.
   ALL RIGHT, LITTLE HONEY BEE.

3. I HEAR A LOT OF BUZZING. SOUNDS LIKE MY LITTLE HONEY BEE.
   I HEAR A LOT OF BUZZING. SOUNDS LIKE MY LITTLE HONEY BEE.
   SHE BEEN ALL AROUND THE WORLD MAKIN' HONEY,
   BUT NOW SHE IS COMIN' BACK HOME TO ME.

I Can't Be Satisfied

Written by Muddy Waters

Additional Lyrics

2. Well, I feel like snappin'
   Pistol in your face.
   I'm gonna let some graveyard
   Lord, be her resting place.
   Woman, I'm troubled, I be all worried in mind.
   Well, baby, I can never be satisfied
   And I just can't keep from cryin'.

3. Well, now, all in my sleep,
   Hear my doorbell ring.
   Lookin' for my baby,
   I didn't see not a dog-gone thing.
   I was troubled, I was all worried in mind.
   Well, honey, I could never be satisfied
   And I just couldn't keep from cryin'.

Optional Lyrics

Well, I know my little old baby,
She gonna jump and shout.
That old train be late, man,
Lord, and I come walkin' out.
I mean trouble, I be all worried in mind.
Well, honey, ain't no way in the world for me to be satisfied
And I just can't keep from cryin'.

I'm Ready

Written by Willie Dixon

Solos

Additional Lyrics

2. All you pretty little chicks with your curly hair,
I know you feel like I ain't nowhere.
But stop what you're doin', baby, come over here.
I'll prove to you, baby, that I ain't no square,
Because I'm ready, as ready's anybody can be.
I am ready for you, I hope you ready for me.

Optional Lyrics

I been drinkin' gin like never before.
I feel so good that I want you to know.
One more drink, I wish you would.
It take a whole lot of lovin' to make me feel good.
Well, I'm ready, as ready's anybody can be.
I am ready for you, I hope you ready for me.

E♭ Version

Mannish Boy
Written by Muddy Waters, Melvin London and Ellas McDaniel

INTRO
Shuffle ♩. = 70

F#7

VERSE
F#7

1. Now when I was young boy,   at the age of five,

my moth-er said I'm gon-na be ___   the great-est man a-live.

But now I'm a man. ___   I made twen-ty - one. ___

I want you be-lieve me, hon-ey,   we have lots of fun.

I'm a man.   I spell "M." ___   "A." ___ child. ___

"N." ___ THAT REP-RE-SENT MAN. NO "B." ___

"O," ___ CHILD, _ "Y," ___ THAT SPELL MAN-NISH BOY.

I'M A MAN. ___ I'M A FULL-GROWN MAN.

I'M A MAN. ___ I'M A ROLL - IN' STONE.

I'M A MAN. ___ I'M A HOOCH-IE COOCH-IE MAN.

VERSE
F#7

2. SIT-TIN' ON THE OUT - SIDE, JUST ME AND MY MATE,

I MADE THE MOON COME UP TWO HOURS _ LATE.

Trouble No More
(Someday Baby)
Written by Muddy Waters

1. Don't care how long you go.

2., 3. See additional lyrics

I don't care how long you stay. ___ But good. kind

Treat - ment, ___ Bring you home some - day. ___

But some - day ba - by, you ain't gon - na trou - ble ___ poor ___

ME AN - Y - MORE.

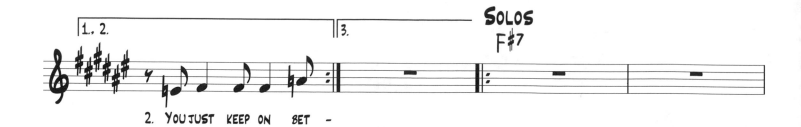

1., 2. | 3. | **SOLOS** F#7

2. YOU JUST KEEP ON BET -

B7

F#7

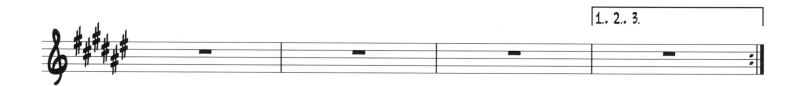

1., 2., 3.

VERSE F#7

4.

4. I'M GON-NA TELL EV - 'RY - BOD - Y   IN YOUR NEIGH - BOR-HOOD

5., 6. See additional lyrics

B7

THAT YOU'RE A SWEET LIT-TLE GIRL

F#7

BUT YOU DON'T MEAN ME NO GOOD.

BUT SOME - DAY, BA - BY, YOU AIN'T GON - NA

TROU - BLE POOR ME AN - Y - MORE.

1., 2.   3.

5. I KNOW YOU'RE

Additional Lyrics

2. You just keep on bettin'
That the dice won't pass.
Well you know, darlin'
You are livin' too fast.
But someday, baby,
you ain't gonna trouble
Poor me anymore.

3. I'm gonna tell ev'rybody
In your neighborhood
That you're a sweet little girl
But you don't mean me no good.
But someday, baby,
you ain't gonna trouble
Poor me anymore.

5. I know you're leaving.
You call that gone.
Oh, without my love
You can't stay long.
But someday, baby,
You ain't gonna trouble
Poor me anymore.

6. Well, goodbye, baby.
Come on, shake my hand.
I don't want no woman
You can have a man.
But someday, baby,
You ain't gonna trouble
Poor me anymore.

Rollin' Stone
(Catfish Blues)
Written by Muddy Waters

Slow Blues ♩. = 67

C#7

1. WELL I WISH _____ I WAS A CAT - FISH SWIM-MIN' IN

2., 3. See additional lyrics

A WHOLE _____ DEEP BLUE SEA. _____ I WILL HAVE ALL

YOU GOOD LOOK - IN' WOM-EN _____ FISH - IN', FISH - IN' AF-TER ME.

SURE 'NOUGH _ AF-TER ME. SURE 'NOUGH _ AF-TER ME. _____

OH, LORD. _____ OH, LORD. _____

SURE 'NOUGH. _____

To Coda ⊕

2. I WENT TO _____

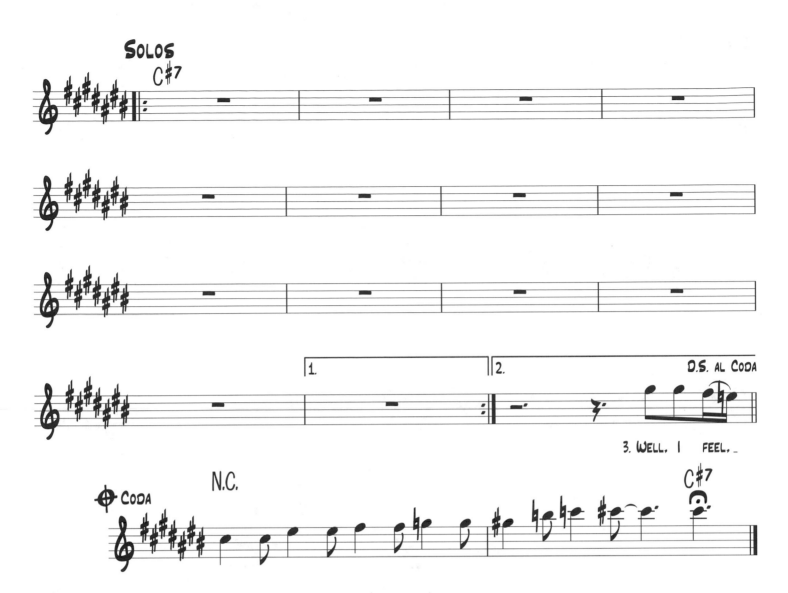

ADDITIONAL LYRICS

2. I WENT TO MY BABY'S HOUSE
   AND I SIT DOWN, HO, ON HER STEP.
   SHE SAID, "COME ON IN, NOW, MUDDY.
   YOU KNOW MY HUSBAND JUST NOW LEFT.
   SURE ENOUGH, HE JUST NOW LEFT.
   SURE ENOUGH, HE JUST NOW LEFT."
   OH, LORD. OH WELL, OH WELL.

3. WELL, I FEEL, YES, I FEEL,
   BABY, LIKE THE LOW DOWN, HO, TIME AIN'T LONG.
   I'M GONNA CATCH THE FIRST THING SMOKIN',
   BACK, BACK DOWN THE ROAD I'M GOING.
   BACK DOWN THE ROAD I'M GOING.
   BACK DOWN THE ROAD I'M GOING.
   SURE ENOUGH, EH. SURE ENOUGH, EH.

OPTIONAL LYRICS

WELL, MY MOTHER TOLD MY FATHER
JUST BEFORE, HMM, I WAS BORN,
"I GOT A BOY CHILD'S COMIN'
HE'S GONNA BE A ROLLIN' STONE.
SURE ENOUGH, HE'S A ROLLIN' STONE.
SURE ENOUGH, HE'S A ROLLIN' STONE.
OH WELL HE'S A, OH WELL HE'S A, OH WELL HE'S A."

CD TRACK

You Shook Me

Words and Music by Willie Dixon and J.B. Lenoir

◆ 8 Full Stereo Mix

◆ 16 Split Mix

E♭ Version

1. You know you shook me, ba - by.

2., 3. See additional lyrics

You shook me all _____ night long. _____

You know you shook me, ba - by.

You shook me all _____ night long. _____

Oh, _____ you kept on shak-in' me, dar-lin',

'til you done messed up _____ my ___ hap-py home.

2. You know you move ___

Solos

3. Oh, _____

Additional Lyrics

2. You know you move me, baby,
   Just like a hurricane.
   You know you moved me, baby,
   Just like a hurricane.
   Oh, you know you move me, darling,
   Just like an earthquake moves the land.

3. Oh, sometime I wonder
   What my poor wife and child's gonna do.
   Oh, sometime I wonder
   What my poor wife and child's gonna do.
   Oh, you know you made me mistreat them, darling.
   Oh, I'm madly in love with you.

🎼 C Version

Good Morning Little Schoolgirl

Words and Music by
Willie Williamson

Additional Lyrics

2. Sometime I don't know what, sometime I don't know what,
   Woman, what in this world to, woman, what in this world to do.
   I don't want to hurt your feeling, Honey, and Muddy don't get mad at you.

3. I'm gonna buy me an airplane, I'm gonna buy me an airplane,
   I'm gonna fly all over Shanty Land, I'm gonna fly all over Shanty Land Town.
   If I don't find my sweet woman, I ain't gonna let my airplane down.

Optional Lyrics

Come on, be my baby. Come on, be my baby.
I'll buy you a diamond, I'll buy you a diamond ring.
If you don't be my baby, Sunshine, I ain't gonna buy you a dog-gone thing.

Honey Bee
Written by Muddy Waters

INTRO
SLOW BLUES ♩. = 62

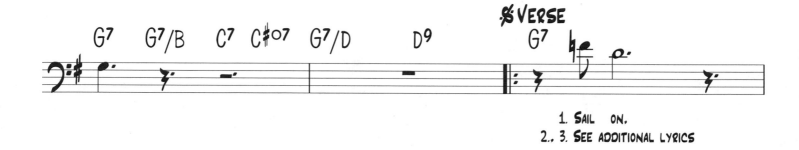

1. Sail on.
2., 3. See additional lyrics

Sail on, my lit-tle hon-ey bee, sail on.

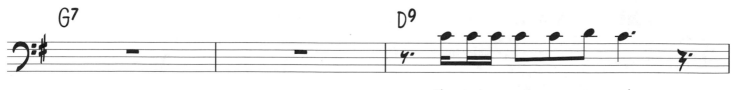

Sail on.   Sail ___ on, my lit-tle hon-ey bee, sail on.

You gon-na keep on sail - in'

TILL YOU LOSE _____ YOUR HAP-PY HOME.

Additional Lyrics

2. SAIL ON, SAIL ON, MY LITTLE HONEY BEE, SAIL ON.
   SAIL ON, SAIL ON, MY LITTLE HONEY BEE, SAIL ON.
   I DON'T MIND YOU SAILIN', BUT PLEASE DON'T SAIL SO LONG.
   ALL RIGHT, LITTLE HONEY BEE.

3. I HEAR A LOT OF BUZZING, SOUNDS LIKE MY LITTLE HONEY BEE.
   I HEAR A LOT OF BUZZING, SOUNDS LIKE MY LITTLE HONEY BEE.
   SHE BEEN ALL AROUND THE WORLD MAKIN' HONEY,
   BUT NOW SHE IS COMIN' BACK HOME TO ME.

I Can't Be Satisfied

Written by Muddy Waters

JUST CAN'T BE SAT-IS-FIED AND I JUST ___ CAN'T ___ KEEP FROM

CRY'N'.

2. WELL, ___ I ___

SOLOS

3. WELL, ___ NOW, ___

ADDITIONAL LYRICS

2. WELL, I FEEL LIKE SNAPPIN'
   PISTOL IN YOUR FACE.
   I'M GONNA LET SOME GRAVEYARD
   LORD, BE HER RESTING PLACE.
   WOMAN, I'M TROUBLED, I BE ALL WORRIED IN MIND.
   WELL, BABY, I CAN NEVER BE SATISFIED
   AND I JUST CAN'T KEEP FROM CRYIN'.

3. WELL, NOW, ALL IN MY SLEEP,
   HEAR MY DOORBELL RING.
   LOOKIN' FOR MY BABY,
   I DIDN'T SEE NOT A DOG-GONE THING.
   I WAS TROUBLED, I WAS ALL WORRIED IN MIND.
   WELL, HONEY, I COULD NEVER BE SATISFIED
   AND I JUST COULDN'T KEEP FROM CRYIN'.

OPTIONAL LYRICS

WELL, I KNOW MY LITTLE OLD BABY,
SHE GONNA JUMP AND SHOUT.
THAT OLD TRAIN BE LATE, MAN,
LORD, AND I COME WALKIN' OUT.
I MEAN TROUBLE, I BE ALL WORRIED IN MIND.
WELL, HONEY, AIN'T NO WAY IN THE WORLD FOR ME TO BE SATISFIED
AND I JUST CAN'T KEEP FROM CRYIN'.

I'm Ready

Written by Willie Dixon

DY - NA - MITE.   I HOPE SOME __ SCREW-BALL   START A FIGHT,   BE-CAUSE I'M

READ-Y,   READ-Y AS AN - Y-BOD-Y CAN BE.   I AM

READ-Y FOR YOU.   I HOPE YOU READ-Y FOR ME.

Solos

2. ALL   YOU

Additional Lyrics

2. ALL YOU PRETTY LITTLE CHICKS WITH YOUR CURLY HAIR,
I KNOW YOU FEEL LIKE I AIN'T NOWHERE.
BUT STOP WHAT YOU'RE DOIN', BABY, COME OVER HERE.
I'LL PROVE TO YOU, BABY, THAT I AIN'T NO SQUARE,
BECAUSE I'M READY, AS READY'S ANYBODY CAN BE.
I AM READY FOR YOU, I HOPE YOU READY FOR ME.

Optional Lyrics

I BEEN DRINKIN' GIN LIKE NEVER BEFORE.
I FEEL SO GOOD THAT I WANT YOU TO KNOW.
ONE MORE DRINK, I WISH YOU WOULD.
IT TAKE A WHOLE LOT OF LOVIN' TO MAKE ME FEEL GOOD.
WELL, I'M READY, AS READY'S ANYBODY CAN BE.
I AM READY FOR YOU, I HOPE YOU READY FOR ME.

🎼 C Version

Mannish Boy
Written by Muddy Waters, Melvin London and Ellas McDaniel

"N." _____ THAT REP-RE-SENT MAN. NO "B," _____

"O." _____ CHILD. __ "Y," _____ THAT SPELL MAN-NISH BOY.

I'M A MAN. ___ I'M A FULL-GROWN MAN.

I'M A MAN. ___ I'M A ROLL - IN' STONE.

I'M A MAN. ___ I'M A HOOCH-IE COOCH - IE MAN.

VERSE
A⁷

2. SIT-TIN' ON THE OUT - SIDE. JUST ME AND MY MATE.

I MADE THE MOON COME UP TWO HOURS __ LATE.

Trouble No More
(Someday Baby)
Written by Muddy Waters

INTRO
Moderate Shuffle ♩ = 153

A7

VERSE
A7

1. Don't care how long you go.
2., 3. See additional lyrics

I don't care how long you stay. ___ But good. Kind

D7   A7

TREAT - MENT. _____   BRING YOU HOME SOME - DAY. ___

BUT SOME - DAY   BA - BY,   YOU AIN'T GON-NA TROU - BLE ___ POOR ___

ME _____ AN - Y - MORE.

1., 2.

3.   SOLOS
A7

2. YOU JUST KEEP ON BET -

D7

A7

1., 2., 3.

4.   VERSE
A7

4. I'M GON - NA TELL EV - 'RY - BOD - Y   IN YOUR NEIGH - BOR - HOOD ___
5., 6. SEE ADDITIONAL LYRICS

D7

___   THAT YOU'RE A SWEET LIT - TLE GIRL

BUT YOU DON'T _____ MEAN ME NO GOOD.

BUT SOME - DAY, BA - BY, YOU AIN'T GON - NA

TROU - BLE _____ POOR _____ ME _____ AN - Y - MORE.

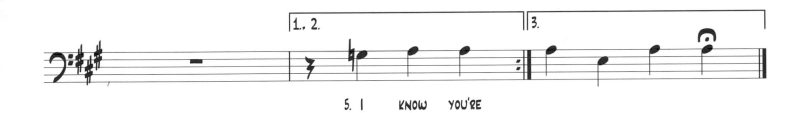

5. I KNOW YOU'RE

Additional Lyrics

2. You just keep on bettin'
That the dice won't pass.
Well you know, darlin'
You are livin' too fast.
But someday, baby,
You ain't gonna trouble
Poor me anymore.

3. I'm gonna tell ev'rybody
In your neighborhood
That you're a sweet little girl
But you don't mean me no good.
But someday, baby,
You ain't gonna trouble
Poor me anymore.

5. I know you're leaving.
You call that gone.
Oh, without my love
You can't stay long.
But someday, baby,
You ain't gonna trouble
Poor me anymore.

6. Well, goodbye, baby.
Come on, shake my hand.
I don't want no woman
You can have a man.
But someday, baby,
You ain't gonna trouble
Poor me anymore.

C VERSION

Rollin' Stone
(Catfish Blues)
WRITTEN BY MUDDY WATERS

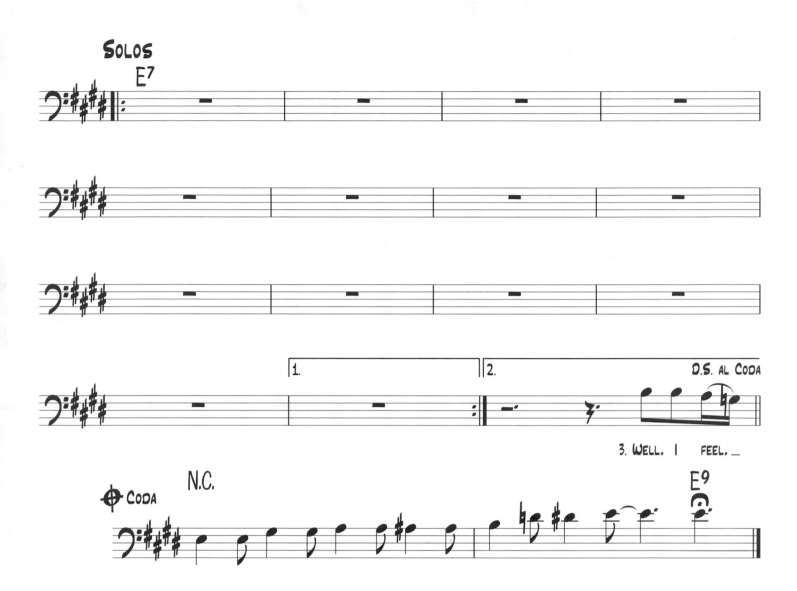

D.S. AL CODA

3. WELL, I FEEL. __

ADDITIONAL LYRICS

2. I WENT TO MY BABY'S HOUSE
   AND I SIT DOWN, HO, ON HER STEP.
   SHE SAID, "COME ON IN, NOW, MUDDY.
   YOU KNOW MY HUSBAND JUST NOW LEFT.
   SURE ENOUGH, HE JUST NOW LEFT.
   SURE ENOUGH, HE JUST NOW LEFT."
   OH, LORD. OH WELL, OH WELL.

3. WELL, I FEEL, YES, I FEEL,
   BABY, LIKE THE LOW DOWN, HO, TIME AIN'T LONG.
   I'M GONNA CATCH THE FIRST THING SMOKIN',
   BACK, BACK DOWN THE ROAD I'M GOING.
   BACK DOWN THE ROAD I'M GOING.
   BACK DOWN THE ROAD I'M GOING.
   SURE ENOUGH, EH. SURE ENOUGH, EH.

OPTIONAL LYRICS

WELL, MY MOTHER TOLD MY FATHER
JUST BEFORE, HMM, I WAS BORN,
"I GOT A BOY CHILD'S COMIN'
HE'S GONNA BE A ROLLIN' STONE.
SURE ENOUGH, HE'S A ROLLIN' STONE.
SURE ENOUGH, HE'S A ROLLIN' STONE.
OH WELL HE'S A, OH WELL HE'S A, OH WELL HE'S A."

You Shook Me

Words and Music by Willie Dixon and J.B. Lenoir

Intro
Slow Blues ♩. = 68

1. You know you shook me, ba - by.

2., 3. See additional lyrics

You shook me all _____ night long. _____

You know you shook me, ba - by.

You shook me all _____ night long. _____

OH, _____ YOU KEPT ON SHAK - IN' ME, DAR - LIN',

'TIL YOU DONE MESSED UP _____ MY ___ HAP - PY HOME.

2. YOU KNOW YOU MOVE __

3. OH, _____

ADDITIONAL LYRICS

2. YOU KNOW YOU MOVE ME, BABY,
   JUST LIKE A HURRICANE.
   YOU KNOW YOU MOVED ME, BABY,
   JUST LIKE A HURRICANE.
   OH, YOU KNOW YOU MOVE ME, DARLING,
   JUST LIKE AN EARTHQUAKE MOVES THE LAND.

3. OH, SOMETIME I WONDER
   WHAT MY POOR WIFE AND CHILD'S GONNA DO.
   OH, SOMETIME I WONDER
   WHAT MY POOR WIFE AND CHILD'S GONNA DO.
   OH, YOU KNOW YOU MADE ME MISTREAT THEM, DARLING,
   OH, I'M MADLY IN LOVE WITH YOU.

HAL·LEONARD
BLUES PLAY-ALONG

For use with all the C, B♭, Bass Clef and E♭ Instruments, the Hal Leonard Blues Play-Along Series is the ultimate jamming tool for all blues musicians.

With easy-to-read lead sheets, and other split-track choices on the included CD, these first-of-a-kind packages will bring your local blues jam right into your house! Each song on the CD includes two tracks: a full stereo mix, and a split track mix with removable guitar, bass, piano, and harp parts. The CD is playable on any CD player, and is also enhanced so Mac and PC users can adjust the recording to any tempo without changing the pitch!

1. Chicago Blues
All Your Love (I Miss Loving) • Easy Baby • I Ain't Got You • I'm Your Hoochie Coochie Man • Killing Floor • Mary Had a Little Lamb • Messin' with the Kid • Sweet Home Chicago.
00843106 Book/CD Pack $12.99

2. Texas Blues
Hide Away • If You Love Me Like You Say • Mojo Hand • Okie Dokie Stomp • Pride and Joy • Reconsider Baby • T-Bone Shuffle • The Things That I Used to Do.
00843107 Book/CD Pack $12.99

3. Slow Blues
Don't Throw Your Love on Me So Strong • Five Long Years • I Can't Quit You Baby • I Just Want to Make Love to You • The Sky Is Crying • (They Call It) Stormy Monday (Stormy Monday Blues) • Sweet Little Angel • Texas Flood.
00843108 Book/CD Pack $12.99

4. Shuffle Blues
Beautician Blues • Bright Lights, Big City • Further on up the Road • I'm Tore Down • Juke • Let Me Love You Baby • Look at Little Sister • Rock Me Baby.
00843171 Book/CD Pack $12.99

5. B.B. King
Everyday I Have the Blues • It's My Own Fault Darlin' • Just Like a Woman • Please Accept My Love • Sweet Sixteen • The Thrill Is Gone • Why I Sing the Blues • You Upset Me Baby.
00843172 Book/CD Pack $14.99

6. Jazz Blues
Birk's Works • Blues in the Closet • Cousin Mary • Freddie Freeloader • Now's the Time • Tenor Madness • Things Ain't What They Used to Be • Turnaround.
00843175 Book/CD Pack $12.99

7. Howlin' Wolf
Built for Comfort • Forty-Four • How Many More Years • Killing Floor • Moanin' at Midnight • Shake for Me • Sitting on Top of the World • Smokestack Lightning.
00843176 Book/CD Pack $12.99

8. Blues Classics
Baby, Please Don't Go • Boom Boom • Born Under a Bad Sign • Dust My Broom • How Long, How Long Blues • I Ain't Superstitious • It Hurts Me Too • My Babe.
00843177 Book/CD Pack $12.99

9. Albert Collins
Brick • Collins' Mix • Don't Lose Your Cool • Frost Bite • Frosty • I Ain't Drunk • Master Charge • Trash Talkin'.
00843178 Book/CD Pack $12.99

10. Uptempo Blues
Cross Road Blues (Crossroads) • Give Me Back My Wig • Got My Mo Jo Working • The House Is Rockin' • Paying the Cost to Be the Boss • Rollin' and Tumblin' • Turn on Your Love Light • You Can't Judge a Book by the Cover.
00843179 Book/CD Pack $12.99

11. Christmas Blues
Back Door Santa • Blue Christmas • Dig That Crazy Santa Claus • Merry Christmas, Baby • Please Come Home for Christmas • Santa Baby • Soulful Christmas.
00843203 Book/CD Pack $12.99

12. Jimmy Reed
Ain't That Lovin' You Baby • Baby, What You Want Me to Do • Big Boss Man • Bright Lights, Big City • Going to New York • Honest I Do • You Don't Have to Go • You Got Me Dizzy.
00843204 Book/CD Pack $12.99

FOR MORE INFORMATION, SEE YOUR LOCAL MUSIC DEALER, OR WRITE TO:

HAL·LEONARD® CORPORATION
7777 W. BLUEMOUND RD. P.O. BOX 13819 MILWAUKEE, WI 53213

Prices, content, and availability subject to change without notice.

www.halleonard.com

1111

ARTIST TRANSCRIPTIONS®

Artist Transcriptions are authentic, note-for-note transcriptions of today's hottest artists in jazz, pop and rock. These outstanding, accurate arrangements are in an easy-to-read format which includes all essential lines. **Artist Transcriptions** can be used to perform, sequence or for reference.

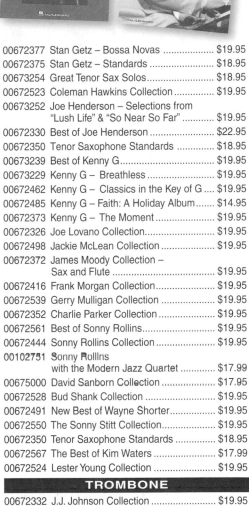

CLARINET

00672423	Buddy De Franco Collection	$19.95

FLUTE

00672379	Eric Dolphy Collection	$19.95
00672582	The Very Best of James Galway	$16.99
00672372	James Moody Collection – Sax and Flute	$19.95

GUITAR & BASS

00660113	The Guitar Style of George Benson	$14.95
00699072	Guitar Book of Pierre Bensusan	$29.95
00672331	Ron Carter – Acoustic Bass	$16.95
00672307	Stanley Clarke Collection	$19.95
00660115	Al Di Meola – Friday Night in San Francisco	$14.95
00604043	Al Di Meola – Music, Words, Pictures	$14.95
00672574	Al Di Meola – Pursuit of Radical Rhapsody	$22.99
00673245	Jazz Style of Tal Farlow	$19.95
00699306	Jim Hall – Exploring Jazz Guitar	$19.95
00604049	Allan Holdsworth – Reaching for the Uncommon Chord	$14.95
00699215	Leo Kottke – Eight Songs	$14.95
00675536	Wes Montgomery – Guitar Transcriptions	$17.95
00672353	Joe Pass Collection	$18.95
00673216	John Patitucci	$16.95
00027083	Django Reinhardt Antholog	$14.95
00026711	Genius of Django Reinhardt	$10.95
00672374	Johnny Smith Guitar Solos	$19.99

PIANO & KEYBOARD

00672338	Monty Alexander Collection	$19.95
00672487	Monty Alexander Plays Standards	$19.95
00672520	Count Basie Collection	$19.95
00672439	Cyrus Chestnut Collection	$19.95
00672300	Chick Corea – Paint the World	$12.95
14037739	Storyville Presents Duke Ellington	$19.99
00672537	Bill Evans at Town Hall	$16.95
00672548	The Mastery of Bill Evans	$12.95
00672425	Bill Evans – Piano Interpretations	$19.95
00672365	Bill Evans – Piano Standards	$19.95
00672510	Bill Evans Trio – Vol. 1: 1959-1961	$24.95
00672511	Bill Evans Trio – Vol. 2: 1962-1965	$24.95
00672512	Bill Evans Trio – Vol. 3: 1968-1974	$24.95
00672513	Bill Evans Trio – Vol. 4: 1979-1980	$24.95
00672381	Tommy Flanagan Collection	$24.99
00672492	Benny Goodman Collection	$16.95
00672486	Vince Guaraldi Collection	$19.95
00672419	Herbie Hancock Collection	$19.95
00672438	Hampton Hawes	$19.95
14037738	Storyville Presents Earl Hines	$19.99
00672322	Ahmad Jamal Collection	$22.95
00672564	Best of Jeff Lorber	$17.99
00672476	Brad Mehldau Collection	$19.99
00672388	Best of Thelonious Monk	$19.95
00672389	Thelonious Monk Collection	$19.95

00672390	Thelonious Monk Plays Jazz Standards – Volume 1	$19.95
00672391	Thelonious Monk Plays Jazz Standards – Volume 2	$19.95
00672433	Jelly Roll Morton – The Piano Rolls	$12.95
00672553	Charlie Parker for Piano	$19.95
00672542	Oscar Peterson – Jazz Piano Solos	$16.95
00672562	Oscar Peterson – A Jazz Portrait of Frank Sinatra	$19.95
00672544	Oscar Peterson – Originals	$9.95
00672532	Oscar Peterson – Plays Broadway	$19.95
00672531	Oscar Peterson – Plays Duke Ellington	$19.95
00672563	Oscar Peterson – A Royal Wedding Suite	$19.99
00672533	Oscar Peterson – Trios	$24.95
00672543	Oscar Peterson Trio – Canadiana Suite	$10.99
00672534	Very Best of Oscar Peterson	$22.95
00672371	Bud Powell Classics	$19.95
00672376	Bud Powell Collection	$19.95
00672507	Gonzalo Rubalcaba Collection	$19.95
00672303	Horace Silver Collection	$19.95
00672316	Art Tatum Collection	$22.95
00672355	Art Tatum Solo Book	$19.95
00672357	Billy Taylor Collection	$24.95
00673215	McCoy Tyner	$16.95
00672321	Cedar Walton Collection	$19.95
00672519	Kenny Werner Collection	$19.95
00672434	Teddy Wilson Collection	$19.95
14037740	Storyville Presents Teddy Wilson	$19.99

SAXOPHONE

00672566	The Mindi Abair Collection	$14.99
00673244	Julian "Cannonball" Adderley Collection	$19.95
00673237	Michael Brecker	$19.95
00672429	Michael Brecker Collection	$19.95
00672315	Benny Carter Plays Standards	$22.95
00672394	James Carter Collection	$19.95
00672349	John Coltrane Plays Giant Steps	$19.95
00672529	John Coltrane – Giant Steps	$14.99
00672494	John Coltrane – A Love Supreme	$14.95
00307393	John Coltrane – Omnibook: C Instruments	$24.99
00307391	John Coltrane – Omnibook: B-flat Instruments	$19.99
00307392	John Coltrane – Omnibook: E-flat Instruments	$24.99
00307394	John Coltrane – Omnibook: Bass Clef Instruments	$24.99
00672493	John Coltrane Plays "Coltrane Changes"	$19.95
00672453	John Coltrane Plays Standards	$19.95
00673233	John Coltrane Solos	$22.95
00672328	Paul Desmond Collection	$19.95
00672379	Eric Dolphy Collection	$19.95
00672530	Kenny Garrett Collection	$19.95
00699375	Stan Getz	$19.95

00672377	Stan Getz – Bossa Novas	$19.95
00672375	Stan Getz – Standards	$18.95
00673254	Great Tenor Sax Solos	$18.95
00672523	Coleman Hawkins Collection	$19.95
00673252	Joe Henderson – Selections from "Lush Life" & "So Near So Far"	$19.95
00672330	Best of Joe Henderson	$22.95
00672350	Tenor Saxophone Standards	$18.95
00673239	Best of Kenny G	$19.95
00673229	Kenny G – Breathless	$19.95
00672462	Kenny G – Classics in the Key of G	$19.95
00672485	Kenny G – Faith: A Holiday Album	$14.95
00672373	Kenny G – The Moment	$19.95
00672326	Joe Lovano Collection	$19.95
00672498	Jackie McLean Collection	$19.95
00672372	James Moody Collection – Sax and Flute	$19.95
00672416	Frank Morgan Collection	$19.95
00672539	Gerry Mulligan Collection	$19.95
00672352	Charlie Parker Collection	$19.95
00672561	Best of Sonny Rollins	$19.95
00672444	Sonny Rollins Collection	$19.95
00102751	Sonny Rollins with the Modern Jazz Quartet	$17.99
00675000	David Sanborn Collection	$17.95
00672528	Bud Shank Collection	$19.95
00672491	New Best of Wayne Shorter	$19.95
00672550	The Sonny Stitt Collection	$19.95
00672350	Tenor Saxophone Standards	$18.95
00672567	The Best of Kim Waters	$17.99
00672524	Lester Young Collection	$19.95

TROMBONE

00672332	J.J. Johnson Collection	$19.95
00672489	Steve Turré Collection	$19.99

TRUMPET

00672557	Herb Alpert Collection	$14.99
00672480	Louis Armstrong Collection	$17.95
00672481	Louis Armstrong Plays Standards	$17.95
00672435	Chet Baker Collection	$19.95
00672556	Best of Chris Botti	$19.95
00672448	Miles Davis – Originals, Vol. 1	$19.95
00672451	Miles Davis – Originals, Vol. 2	$19.95
00672450	Miles Davis – Standards, Vol. 1	$19.95
00672449	Miles Davis – Standards, Vol. 2	$19.95
00672479	Dizzy Gillespie Collection	$19.95
00673214	Freddie Hubbard	$14.95
00672382	Tom Harrell – Jazz Trumpet	$19.95
00672363	Jazz Trumpet Solos	$9.95
00672506	Chuck Mangione Collection	$19.95
00672525	Arturo Sandoval – Trumpet Evolution	$19.95

HAL•LEONARD® CORPORATION

7777 W. BLUEMOUND RD. P.O. BOX 13819 MILWAUKEE, WI 53213

Visit our web site for a complete listing of our titles with songlists at

www.halleonard.com

0913

Prices and availability subject to change without notice.

Presenting the Hal Leonard JAZZ PLAY-ALONG SERIES

For use with all B-flat, E-flat, Bass Clef and C instruments, the Jazz Play-Along® Series is the ultimate learning tool for all jazz musicians. With musician-friendly lead sheets, melody cues, and other split-track choices on the included CD, these first-of-a-kind packages help you master improvisation while playing some of the greatest tunes of all time. FOR STUDY, each tune includes a split track with: melody cue with proper style and inflection • professional rhythm tracks • choruses for soloing • removable bass part • removable piano part. FOR PERFORMANCE, each tune also has: an additional full stereo accompaniment track (no melody) • additional choruses for soloing.

73. **JAZZ/BLUES** 00843075 .... $14.95	107. **MOTOWN CLASSICS** 00843116 .... $14.99	143. **JUST THE BLUES** 00843223 .... $15.99
74. **BEST JAZZ CLASSICS** 00843076 .... $15.99	108. **JAZZ WALTZ** 00843159 .... $15.99	144. **LEE MORGAN** 00843229 .... $15.99
75. **PAUL DESMOND** 00843077 .... $16.99	109. **OSCAR PETERSON** 00843160 .... $16.99	145. **COUNTRY STANDARDS** 00843230 .... $15.99
76. **BROADWAY JAZZ BALLADS** 00843078 .... $15.99	110. **JUST STANDARDS** 00843161 .... $15.99	146. **RAMSEY LEWIS** 00843231 .... $15.99
77. **JAZZ ON BROADWAY** 00843079 .... $15.99	111. **COOL CHRISTMAS** 00843162 .... $15.99	147. **SAMBA** 00843232 .... $15.99
78. **STEELY DAN** 00843070 .... $15.99	112. **PAQUITO D'RIVERA – LATIN JAZZ*** 48020662 .... $16.99	150. **JAZZ IMPROV BASICS** 00843195 .... $19.99
79. **MILES DAVIS CLASSICS** 00843081 .... $15.99	113. **PAQUITO D'RIVERA – BRAZILIAN JAZZ*** 48020663 .... $19.99	151. **MODERN JAZZ QUARTET CLASSICS** 00843209 .... $15.99
80. **JIMI HENDRIX** 00843083 .... $16.99	114. **MODERN JAZZ QUARTET FAVORITES** 00843163 .... $15.99	152. **J.J. JOHNSON** 00843210 .... $15.99
81. **FRANK SINATRA – CLASSICS** 00843084 .... $15.99	115. **THE SOUND OF MUSIC** 00843164 .... $15.99	154. **HENRY MANCINI** 00843213 .... $14.99
82. **FRANK SINATRA – STANDARDS** 00843085 .... $16.99	116. **JACO PASTORIUS** 00843165 .... $15.99	155. **SMOOTH JAZZ CLASSICS** 00843215 .... $15.99
83. **ANDREW LLOYD WEBBER** 00843104 .... $14.95	117. **ANTONIO CARLOS JOBIM – MORE HITS** 00843166 .... $15.99	156. **THELONIOUS MONK – EARLY GEMS** 00843216 .... $15.99
84. **BOSSA NOVA CLASSICS** 00843105 .... $14.95	118. **BIG JAZZ STANDARDS COLLECTION** 00843167 .... $27.50	157. **HYMNS** 00843217 .... $15.99
85. **MOTOWN HITS** 00843109 .... $14.95	119. **JELLY ROLL MORTON** 00843168 .... $15.99	158. **JAZZ COVERS ROCK** 00843219 .... $15.99
86. **BENNY GOODMAN** 00843110 .... $15.99	120. **J.S. BACH** 00843169 .... $15.99	159. **MOZART** 00843220 .... $15.99
87. **DIXIELAND** 00843111 .... $16.99	121. **DJANGO REINHARDT** 00843170 .... $15.99	160. **GEORGE SHEARING** 14041531 .... $16.99
88. **DUKE ELLINGTON FAVORITES** 00843112 .... $14.95	122. **PAUL SIMON** 00843182 .... $16.99	161. **DAVE BRUBECK** 14041556 .... $16.99
89. **IRVING BERLIN FAVORITES** 00843113 .... $14.95	123. **BACHARACH & DAVID** 00843185 .... $15.99	162. **BIG CHRISTMAS COLLECTION** 00843221 .... $24.99
90. **THELONIOUS MONK CLASSICS** 00841262 .... $16.99	124. **JAZZ-ROCK HORN HITS** 00843186 .... $15.99	164. **HERB ALPERT** 14041775 .... $16.99
91. **THELONIOUS MONK FAVORITES** 00841263 .... $16.99	126. **COUNT BASIE CLASSICS** 00843157 .... $15.99	165. **GEORGE BENSON** 00843240 .... $16.99
92. **LEONARD BERNSTEIN** 00450134 .... $15.99	127. **CHUCK MANGIONE** 00843188 .... $15.99	167. **JOHNNY MANDEL** 00103642 .... $16.99
93. **DISNEY FAVORITES** 00843142 .... $14.99	128. **VOCAL STANDARDS (LOW VOICE)** 00843189 .... $15.99	168. **TADD DAMERON** 00103663 .... $15.99
94. **RAY** 00843143 .... $14.99	129. **VOCAL STANDARDS (HIGH VOICE)** 00843190 .... $15.99	169. **BEST JAZZ STANDARDS** 00109249 .... $19.99
95. **JAZZ AT THE LOUNGE** 00843144 .... $14.99	130. **VOCAL JAZZ (LOW VOICE)** 00843191 .... $15.99	170. **ULTIMATE JAZZ STANDARDS** 00109250 .... $19.99
96. **LATIN JAZZ STANDARDS** 00843145 .... $15.99	131. **VOCAL JAZZ (HIGH VOICE)** 00843192 .... $15.99	172. **POP STANDARDS** 00111669 .... $15.99
97. **MAYBE I'M AMAZED*** 00843148 .... $15.99	132. **STAN GETZ ESSENTIALS** 00843193 .... $15.99	174. **TIN PAN ALLEY** 00119125 .... $15.99
98. **DAVE FRISHBERG** 00843149 .... $15.99	133. **STAN GETZ FAVORITES** 00843194 .... $15.99	175. **TANGO** 00119836 .... $15.99
99. **SWINGING STANDARDS** 00843150 .... $14.99	134. **NURSERY RHYMES*** 00843196 .... $17.99	176. **JOHNNY MERCER** 00119838 .... $15.99
100. **LOUIS ARMSTRONG** 00740423 .... $16.99	135. **JEFF BECK** 00843197 .... $15.99	
101. **BUD POWELL** 00843152 .... $14.99	136. **NAT ADDERLEY** 00843198 .... $15.99	
102. **JAZZ POP** 00843153 .... $15.99	137. **WES MONTGOMERY** 00843199 .... $15.99	
103. **ON GREEN DOLPHIN STREET & OTHER JAZZ CLASSICS** 00843154 .... $14.99	138. **FREDDIE HUBBARD** 00843200 .... $15.99	
104. **ELTON JOHN** 00843155 .... $14.99	139. **JULIAN "CANNONBALL" ADDERLEY** 00843201 .... $15.99	
105. **SOULFUL JAZZ** 00843151 .... $15.99	140. **JOE ZAWINUL** 00843202 .... $15.99	
106. **SLO' JAZZ** 00843117 .... $14.99	141. **BILL EVANS STANDARDS** 00843156 .... $15.99	
	142. **CHARLIE PARKER GEMS** 00843222 .... $15.99	

*These CDs do not include split tracks.

1013